DORLING KINDERSLEY *TRAVEL GUIDES*

KIDS' LONDON

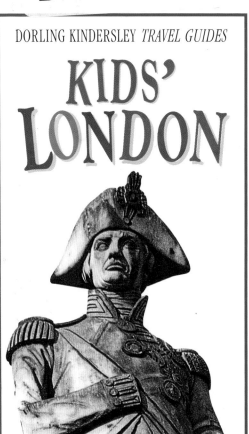

DORLING KINDERSLEY *TRAVEL GUIDES*

KIDS'
LONDON

SIMON ADAMS

A Dorling Kindersley Book

DORLING KINDERSLEY
London • New York • Sydney • Delhi
Paris • Munich • Johannesburg

Senior Editor Giles Sparrow
Senior Art Editor Cheryl Telfer
Editor Kathleen Bada
Designer Darren Holt

Managing Editor Jayne Parsons
Managing Art Editor Gillian Shaw

DTP Designer Nomazwe Madonko
Picture Researcher Samantha Nunn
Jacket Design Dean Price
Production Orla Creegan
US Editor Chuck Wills

First American edition, 2000
2 4 6 8 10 9 7 5 3 1

Published in the United States by
Dorling Kindersley Publishing, Inc.,
95 Madison Avenue,
New York, New York 10016
Copyright © 2000
Dorling Kindersley Limited, London

Library of Congress Cataloguing-in-Publication Data
Kids' London.-- 1st American ed.
p. cm. -- (Dorling Kindersley travel guides)
Includes index.
Summary: A travel guide that focuses on the major sights of
London and includes color photographs, listings, and
key facts.
ISBN 0-7894-5249-9
1. London (England)--Guidebooks–Juvenile literature.
2. Children--Travel--England--London--
Guidebooks--[1. London (England)--Guides.]
I. Dorling Kindersley Publishing, Inc. II. Series.
DA679.K47 2000
914.2104'859--dc21
99-055203

Color reproduction by Colourscan, Singapore
Printed and bound in Italy by Graphicom

For a complete catalog visit [DK] www.dk.com

Contents

DOUBLE-DECKER
BUS

BEEFEATER

HARRIER JET

How to use this book

IN THIS BOOK YOU'LL find all the
information you need for a trip
to London. Each page features
a popular sight or attraction. Special
color-coded boxes suggest extra
activities to try, and tell you
fascinating facts about the city.

Maps to help you find key sights.

"Cool for kids" is full of other fun activities in the area or related to the same subject.

"Did you know?" has strange and wacky facts related to the feature.

TREASURE HUNT

❶ Whose plays are
performed in the
Globe Theater?

❷ How many bridges lie
between Westminster and
Tower bridges?

❸ What is the name
of the ship next to
Southwark Cathedral?

"Treasure Hunt" boxes contain quiz questions or unusual objects to look for. Answers are in the back of the book.

SYMBOLS

The Hard Facts box at the foot of each page
contains essential details for each attraction. Symbols
tell you what type of information is being given.

✉ Address	🕐 Opening hours
☎ Telephone number	£ Admission charges
⊖ 🚇 How to get there	**www.** Website address

London calendar

LONDON'S YEAR is packed full of special events, ranging from carnivals and sports to big royal and city ceremonies. Whatever time of year you're in London, there's sure to be something going on!

People spend months preparing their costumes.

PERFORMER IN CARNIVAL DRESS

On the last weekend in August, Afro-Caribbean Londoners throw the biggest party in the country. **Notting Hill Carnival** attracts half a million visitors each year. Try delicious food, dance to the huge sound systems, or just enjoy the sights.

The London Marathon, the world's largest, takes place on a Sunday in mid-April. Over 30,000 people run from Greenwich to Westminster, and tens of thousands more line the route to cheer them along.

FIREWORKS AT TOWER BRIDGE

Remember, remember, the fifth of November! Every year, London celebrates **Bonfire Night**, the anniversary of Guy Fawkes' unsuccessful attempt to blow up Parliament in 1605. Enjoy fireworks galore, bonfires, and the commemorative burning of the Guy!

ANNUAL EVENTS

Chinese New Year: Early February, Chinatown. Dragons dance, cymbals clash!

The Boat Race: Early March. Oxford and Cambridge crews row along the river.

FA Cup Final: Late May, Wembley – or watch it on TV with the rest of the country!

Trooping the Color: Mid-June, Westminster. The Queen's official birthday celebration.

Lord Mayor's Show: Early November. Huge parade through the City, and fireworks!

Christmas Lights: December, West End. See the brilliant street decorations and elaborate shop displays.

Packed and ready

WELCOME TO LONDON, one of the best cities in the world. It's also one of the biggest and busiest, packed with things to do and see. If you want to get the best out of your trip, you'd better plan it in advance, and know how to stay in touch and get help if you need it.

BACKPACK

Look up when you're walking around London - you don't know what you might see! Many buildings display blue plaques, showing that a famous person once lived there. Everyone from writers to rock stars, politicians to poets, is on a wall somewhere. More famous people stand around as statues in the parks and squares.

BINOCULARS

COINS

CAMERA

The complete London tourist needs a camera, a notebook and pen, a good guidebook, and maybe even binoculars – especially if you're planning to climb St. Paul's or go for a ride in the London Eye. You'll need money to buy food, drinks, and presents (for your friends and yourself), and an A–Z street guide is also a must – it's a confusing city!

GREATER LONDON COUNCIL

BRAM STOKER
1847–1912
Author of
"DRACULA"
lived here

CHARLIE CHAPLIN IN LEICESTER SQUARE

Bram Stoker, creator of Dracula, lived in Chelsea.

Police cars and other emergency vehicles have blue flashing lights and sirens – get out of the road if you hear one coming!

- -
DID YOU KNOW?

★ 1p and 2p coins are copper, 5p, 10p, 20p, and 50p are silver, £1 is gold, and £2 is gold and silver. Unfortunately, they're not real gold or silver!

★ Notes are £5, £10, £20, and £50. All notes and coins have a picture of the Queen on one side.
- -

Police, fire, or ambulance services ☎ In an emergency, dial 999 or 112.
If you lose property in the street, contact the police (not by dialing 999!)

Send a postcard to a friend – it doesn't cost much. You can buy stamps and cards in a newsagent or at a post office. If you're sending a card abroad, then don't forget to mark it "Par Avion – By Airmail."

Avoid lines by using these machines at post offices

MAIL BOX

Phone boxes come in two main types. BT boxes are the most common and accept coins or BT phonecards. Boxes run by other companies may only accept their own phonecards. Buy the right cards from a newsagent or post office.

You can buy a plastic policeman's helmet as a souvenir – but don't try to arrest anyone!

TRADITIONAL RED PHONE BOX

NEW STYLE PHONE BOX

BT PHONECARD

Make sure you always have a map with you – London's streets have no logical layout!

If you get lost, or find yourself in trouble, get help from a police officer. They wear a blue uniform, and can be found on foot, in a white police car, or sometimes on horseback. Don't be scared of them – they're there to help you!

London Transport Lost Property ⊖ Baker Street ☎ (020) 7486-2496
Black Cab Lost Property Office ☎ (020) 7833-0996

Getting around

LONDON IS A GREAT CITY to walk around, but it's also very big, so you will often need to take a bus, train, or taxi. London's streets are very confusing and it's easy to get lost; so get a map or, better still, buy an A–Z, which shows every street in the city. Enjoy your visit!

Drive a London bus or control a tube train at the **London Transport Museum** in Covent Garden. The place is packed with historic trams, trains, and buses, and there are lots of buttons to push and computer screens to play with. All aboard!

Careful – some lines split in two!

The London underground, or "tube," is incredibly complex, but the tube map makes it easy. Each line has its own color and name. Plan your route on the map, then follow the colored signs inside the stations to find your platform and train. Watch out for lines that branch!

Almost every part of London has a tube station. Look out for the distinctive red and blue circular sign, buy your ticket, and head down into the depths. The "tube" is often hot, packed, and noisy, but the dark tunnels are fun as you hurtle along under the London streets.

Docklands trains are driverless, so you can sit at the front!

Docklands Light Railway trains have big windows and run on an elevated track like a roller coaster. They'll take you to Greenwich, or past Britain's tallest building at Canary Wharf.

Rush hours are 8 am – 10 am and 5 pm – 7 pm.
London Transport Museum ✉ The Piazza, Covent Garden WC2

When the yellow light is on, the taxi is available for hire.

Travel in style in a black cab! The drivers have to take an exam called "the knowledge," which tests them on routes around London. Provided you stick with a licensed cab (they're not always black, but they always have a yellow "taxi" sign) you should get to where you want to go.

All buses show a route number and a list of stops on the front.

Bus stops show route numbers, directions, and timetables.

Get the best view of London from the top of a **double-decker bus**! Check the front of the bus to make sure it's going the right way, pay your fare to the driver or conductor, then sit back and enjoy the ride – much cheaper than a tour bus!

BUS STOP
Baker Street Station ⊖

towards
Marble Arch

74	82	274
755	757	758
777	796	797

These mini-maps show you where all the buses in the area go to.

Wait by the beacon until the traffic stops.

London's roads are very busy, so always use a pedestrian crossing. Some have a button you have to push, but **"zebra" crossings** have black and white stripes across the road, and flashing orange beacons on either side. The traffic's supposed to stop and allow you to cross, but be careful!

DID YOU KNOW?

★ The first "tube" line opened in 1863. The carriages were pulled by steam engines.

★ The tube has over 250 miles (400 km) of track – the longest underground railroad in the world.

★ The tube map is based on an electrical circuit diagram.

☎ (020) 7379-6344 ⊖ Covent Garden ☺ 10 am – 6 pm (opens 11 am Fri) ⓔ Charge **www.** londontransport.co.uk; www.ltmuseum.co.uk

Westminster

THE MOST POWERFUL people in Britain work in Westminster. The Prime Minister, House of Lords, and Members of Parliament (MPs) meet here, and kings and queens are crowned in the Abbey. Watch the famous come and go, and see what the politicians on television look like in real life!

This ceremonial mace sits in Parliament whenever it meets.

The most famous front door in the world is down a dark and poky street off Whitehall. It's the entrance to **10 Downing Street**, the home of the Prime Minister. Unfortunately, high gates and police officers stop you from getting too close!

BONFIRE NIGHT FIREWORKS

Home of the world

Although the Houses of Parliament look old, they were mostly built less than 150 years ago after a huge fire. In 1605, Guy Fawkes and other plotters tried to blow up Parliament – the people of Britain remember his failure with fireworks and bonfires every November 5.

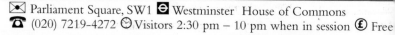

✉ Parliament Square, SW1   ⊖ Westminster   House of Commons
☎ (020) 7219-4272   🕑 Visitors 2:30 pm – 10 pm when in session   £ Free

Brass plaque from a medieval tomb

Every English king and queen since 1066 has been crowned in Westminster Abbey, and many are buried here. In fact, 3,000 people lie beneath its floors.

TREASURE HUNT

1 Which king stands outside the Houses of Parliament?

2 Who lives next door to the Prime Minister?

3 Who are the 10 people who greet you above the entrance to Westminster Abbey?

est-known clock!

The clock face is 23 ft (7 m) across, and each numeral is 2 ft (60 cm) tall.

Take home a souvenir of your visit to **Westminster Abbey** by making a brass rubbing in the Cloisters.

Everyone calls the clocktower that looms high over Parliament **Big Ben**, but in fact this is St. Stephen's Tower. Big Ben is the name of the clock's 14-ton bell, which rings every hour.

COOL FOR KIDS

★ Join the line to see Parliament in action from the Strangers' Gallery.

★ Look out for MPs being interviewed on Parliament Green – you might even get on television!

Westminster Abbey ☎ (020) 7222-5152 ⊘ 9:20 am – 3:45 pm Mon – Fri, 9 am – 1:45 pm Sat £ Charge for some parts **www.** parliament.uk

Trafalgar Square

STAND IN TRAFALGAR SQUARE and it seems as if the whole world has shown up to join you! Tourists, art lovers, diplomats, and Londoners flow in and out of the square all day – why not join them?

Four massive lions guard the base of Nelson's Column. But don't be scared. They're just big bronze pussycats, really, and they don't mind you sitting on their paws.

DID YOU KNOW?

★ 14 stonemasons held a dinner on top of Nelson's Column before the statue was placed there in 1842.

★ Every year, the city of Oslo, Norway, sends over a Christmas tree for the square.

Feed the pigeons! Most birds live in trees, but these pigeons live on roofs, and swoop down into the square to be fed. Buy some seed from the **stall in the square**, and don't be scared when the pigeons turn you into a perch.

Trafalgar Square is the biggest square in central London. Unfortunately, it's surrounded by busy roads, but there are plans to get rid of the cars and make it pedestrian-only.

National Gallery

National Portrait Gallery

Charing Cross Road

St. Martin-in-the-Fields

Nelson's Column

South Africa House

✉ Trafalgar Square WC2
🚇 Charing Cross, Leicester Square

THE AMBASSADORS

The painting shows two 16th-century Frenchmen visiting London.

Nelson was blinded in one eye during battle in 1794.

165ft above London stands Britain's greatest naval hero

The National Gallery contains some of the world's most **famous paintings**. Name an artist, and at least one of his or her works will be here. Some of the paintings are very strange – Hans Holbein's *The Ambassadors* is one of the oddest!

COOL FOR KIDS

★ See the pictures of famous people in the National Portrait Gallery.

★ Go brass rubbing in the crypt of St. Martin-in-the-Fields.

★ Get your photo taken next to a lion.

Stand next to Nelson on top of his column and the streets of London would be 165 ft (50 m) beneath your feet. Horatio Nelson won a famous naval victory against the French at Trafalgar in 1805, which is how the Square got its name, and why Nelson was given a column to stand on!

National Gallery ☎ (020) 7839-3321 ⓔ Free ⊘ 10 am – 6 pm (9 pm Weds) **www.** nationalgallery.org.uk; www.npg.org.uk

Covent Garden & Leicester Square

AS A VISITOR TO LONDON, you won't be alone around here – this is the biggest tourist area in the capital. Lots of things to look at, places to visit, food to eat, and shops to spend your money in. Enjoy!

AUTOMATON FROM COVENT GARDEN

Street performers, opera, movies, eating, shoppi...

See a man eat spaghetti in a bathtub and the strangest submarine you've ever seen! Not as strange as it sounds – they're all automata (mechanical sculptures) in the **Cabaret Mechanical Theatre**.

If you hear someone singing opera from an upstairs window, or catch a glimpse of a ballet dancer, you're probably near the **Royal Opera House**, home to both the Royal Opera and Royal Ballet companies. Take a guided tour, or, better still, get a ticket for a performance.

✉ Covent Garden, WC2; Leicester Square, WC2
Ⓔ Covent Garden, Leicester Square, Piccadilly Circus

Stand in Leicester Square in the early evening, and you might just catch a glimpse of a famous movie star. The square is packed with **theaters**, and if you see crowd barriers going up, you'll know that a big movie is having a star-studded opening tonight.

Old market buildings

COOL FOR KIDS

★ Shop 'til you drop in Covent Garden.

★ Check out the transport and theater museums.

★ See a traditional Punch and Judy show.

★ Hang out with the crowds in the Piazza.

Pagoda gate

Jugglers, unicyclists, mime artists, clowns, human statues, and buskers (street performers) provide all-day entertainment in Covent Garden and Leicester Square. If you get bored with one show, another one will be along shortly!

DID YOU KNOW?

★ Charlie Chaplin, the famous movie comedian whose statue stands in Leicester Square, was born in South London in 1889.

★ Covent Garden used to be London's main fruit and vegetable market until the market moved south of the river in 1974.

Fed up with burgers and fish 'n' chips? Want a taste of the Orient? Then head to London's **Chinatown**, as close to China as you can get without getting on a plane!

☉ Street performers from about 11 am – dusk (later in Leicester Square)

www. covent-garden.co.uk

Piccadilly Circus & West End

IF LONDON HAD A HEART, it would have to be in Piccadilly Circus. Sit on the steps underneath the statue of Eros and chat with your friends, have fun in the Trocadero or Rock Circus, shop for records, clothes or toys, go to the movies, or eat a burger – there's just so much to do in and around Piccadilly!

MADAME TUSSAUD'S
ROCK CIRCUS

Meet your favorite rock star – and all those singers you forgot about long ago – in **Rock Circus**. Hear them sing, read all about them, watch a live concert, and bop 'til you drop!

Stand next to Eros, and most of the surrounding buildings are hidden by the famous neon advertising slogans covering their walls. Even on the darkest night, Piccadilly Circus is never dull.

Eros stands in the middle of the circus.

TREASURE HUNT

❶ Who was Eros?

❷ What does Piccadilly mean?

❸ What is Eros made of?

✉ Piccadilly Circus W1 🚇 Piccadilly Circus, Oxford Circus, Leicester Sq.
Trocadero ⏲ 10 am – midnight daily 💷 Charge for separate attractions

Ever wanted to commentate on a soccer match? Then head for the **BBC Experience** at Broadcasting House! You can also present a weather forecast, record a radio play, and learn all about the world's most famous broadcasting network.

BBC EXPERIENCE

Drop through the floor on the Free Fall Ride, ride the bumper cars in Funland Lazerbowl, test your wits on the video games of Segaworld, or be surrounded by a movie in the IMAX 3D cinema – all in the **Trocadero**. Probably the most fun you can have in a single building in the world!

Entrance to Segaworld

OXFORD STREET

CITY OF WESTMINSTER

TOYS FROM HAMLEY'S

The most famous statue in London stands in the middle of Piccadilly Circus. Everyone calls it **Eros**, but in fact it represents Charity, and was put up to commemorate a famous campaigner against child labor.

Play around in Hamley's on Regent Street, one of the world's best toy stores. There are five floors of fun, with a huge selection of computer and board games, and a video arcade in the basement! Continue to Oxford Street, London's main shopping street.

BBC ☎ (0870) 603-0304 ⊙ 9:30 am – 4:30 pm (1 pm – 4:30 pm Mon)
£ Charge www. segaworld.com; www.bbc.co.uk/experience

A trip to the theater

EVERY EVENING, and some afternoons too, London's theaters are packed with hushed crowds, eager for the show to start. Serious plays, comedies, musicals, and thrillers – take your pick and enjoy some of the best theater in the world!

Cats? Phantom of the Opera? You know the songs, now see the shows they come from. London is the world capital of musicals, and you can't beat a musical for a good night out!

POSTERS AND TICKETS FROM SHOWS

London's Theaterland is centered on the West End, around Covent Garden and Leicester Square. You can get half-price theater tickets on the day of the show from the ticket booth in Leicester Square. It opens at 12 noon and tickets sell fast, so get there early!

Shakespeare's Globe ✉ New Globe Walk SE1 ☎ (020) 7902-1400
Ⓔ Southwark ◷ Museum: 10 am – 5 pm Ⓕ Charge

The New Shakespeare Company's
1999 Season
OPENAIR THEATRE
REGENT'S PARK

The Merry Wives of Windsor

Twelfth Night

A Funny Thing
Happened On
The Way To The Forum

The Last Fattybottypuss
In The World

If the weather is good, there's nothing finer on a summer's evening than sitting on the grass with an ice-cream and watching a play. Several of London's parks have open-air stages, but **Regent's Park's Open Air Theater** is one of the best. Plays put on here range from Shakespeare to family musicals and plays written especially for kids.

COOL FOR KIDS

★ Hang around the stage door after the show ends and get autographs from your favorite actors.

★ Visit the Theater Museum in Covent Garden and learn more about the history of theatre.

Unicorns don't exist, but the Unicorn Theater most definitely does. It is the oldest theater in London for children (or, to put it another way, not for adults) so sit back and enjoy all the best plays, mime, and puppet theater written especially for you.

Hansel and Gretel in a Unicorn Theater play

All the world's a stage! The play's the thing!

Go to the theater Elizabethan style at Shakespeare's Globe in Southwark. In the 1600s, the poorest members of the audience (called groundlings) paid a penny to stand in the theater. Seats cost three cents and were reserved for the rich.

DID YOU KNOW?

★ The longest-running play in the world is Agatha Christie's *The Mousetrap*, a thriller that opened in 1952 and is still going strong at St. Martin's Theater after 19,500 performances.

The Globe Theater is an exact replica of the building where many of William Shakespeare's greatest plays were first staged 400 years ago. The Globe has the first thatched roof built in London since the Great Fire of 1666, but is mostly open to the weather, so plays are only performed in summer. At other times, you can take a tour and learn about the theater's history.

For details of theater in London, check *Time Out* or other listings magazines. **www.** londontheatre.co.uk (note British spelling of "theater"!)

British Museum

DON'T BE MISLED by the name – the British Museum contains historical objects from all over the world. See the Egyptian mummies, then step next door into an Assyrian palace or Roman temple. Tour the world, and enjoy the trip!

The front of the Museum looks like a **Greek temple**, but inside there are also Celtic, Roman, Egyptian, Chinese, and Aztec treasures.

BUCKLE FROM SUTTON HOO

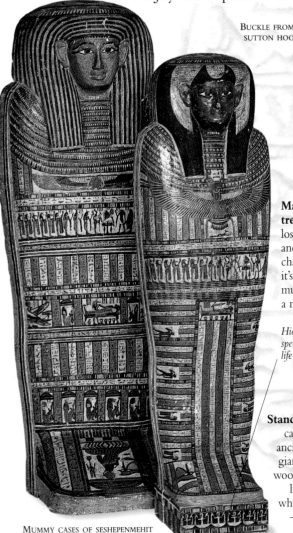

Many of the Museum's treasures were buried or lost for hundreds of years and only turned up by chance. Like the treasures it's easy to get lost in the museum, so pick up a map or guidebook!

Hieroglyphs (picture writing) spell the protective charm "All life and power."

Hunt fo

Stand next to a mummy case and you'd think the ancient Egyptians were all giants. But inside her two wooden cases and layers of linen, Seshepenmehit – who died in about 650BC – was not much bigger than you.

MUMMY CASES OF SESHEPENMEHIT

✉ Great Russell Street, WC1   ☎ (020) 7636-1555
Ⓔ Tottenham Court Road, Holborn, Russell Square

Getting buried in Saxon England was a complex affair. Kings and lords were sometimes buried in ships, surrounded by treasures to take to the afterlife. The man behind this helmet was a 7th-century king buried at **Sutton Hoo** in southeastern England.

Bridge of helmet is a flying duck.

DID YOU KNOW?

★ The British Museum was founded in 1753 and is the biggest museum in Britain.

★ The Museum is the second most popular tourist attraction in Britain, after Blackpool beach. More than 6 million people visit every year!

TREASURE HUNT

❶ Which stone contains three languages?

❷ Name the Egyptian cat goddess.

❸ Who are the Lewis chessmen?

❹ Whose statue stands by the main entrance?

Lindow Man was buried in a peat bog in Cheshire, England, for 2,000 years, until 1984. The newspapers called him "**Pete Marsh,**" and he is so well preserved that scientists know what his last meal was. Lindow Man was strangled to death - perhaps in a ritual sacrifice.

treasure in the heart of London

The Elgin Marbles are not glass balls to play with but stone carvings to admire. They once decorated the temple of the **Parthenon** in Athens, Greece, and show a procession of worshipers walking up the hill to the temple. See them while you can – the Greeks would like them back!

🕐 Mon – Sat 10 am – 5 pm, Sunday 12 pm – 6 pm ⓕ Free
www. british-museum.ac.uk

Buckingham Palace

WHEN YOU ARE QUEEN of England, you get to live in a palace, with grand rooms for balls and banquets, a movie theater, swimming pool, your own post office, a 40-acre walled garden, and a staff of 300 to look after you. Be on you best behavior when you go to visit!

COOL FOR KIDS

★ Look up at the flagpole on top of the building. If the Royal Standard is flying, the Queen is at home.

★ Visit the Royal Mews and see the Queen's horses and the fabulous Gold Carriage.

The Palace is guarded by soldiers in elaborate old-fashioned uniforms. You can watch the **Changing of the Guard**, where the old guard goes off duty and is replaced by new ones, through the railings – it's very impressive, with lots of military precision, foot stamping, and shouting!

Seated on a giant pile of stone outside the Palace is a statue of Queen Victoria. She was queen from 1837–1901, and is the longest-reigning monarch in British history.

Queen Victoria

You can tell the different regiments by the buttons on their coats.

✉ The Mall, SW1 ☎ (020) 7930-4832 🚇 Green Park, St. James's Park
🕐 Changing of the Guard 11:30 am alternate days (every day April – July)

During August and September, join the line to look around the **state rooms** inside. Most are lavishly decorated – this is where the Queen entertains visiting heads of state and other VIPs. But you won't get to meet her, since she spends summer up in Scotland.

When you've seen the Palace and changed the guard, go for a stroll in **St. James's Park**. It's not one of the larger parks in London, but it is certainly the prettiest. Listen to an English brass band on a summer day, or feed the birds – ducks, geese, and pelicans – on the lake.

The original Buckingham Palace was a townhouse built for the Duke of Buckingham in 1703. George III bought the house in 1762 and turned it into the official London residence of the British monarch.

Balcony where the Royal Family appear on special occasions

DID YOU KNOW?

★ The palace is back-to-front: the side you look at from the Mall is the back of the building.

★ Buckingham Palace is the largest private house in London – it has more than 660 rooms.

⊙ State rooms open 9:30 am – 4:15 pm Tues – Sun (Aug – Sept only)
ⓔ Charge **www.** royal.gov.uk

Hyde Park

HAD ENOUGH OF CROWDS of people? Then head to Hyde Park, a huge stretch of open grass and trees in the center of London. Part of the park, called Kensington Gardens, is full of statues and fountains, but the whole place is packed with interesting things to do and see.

Statue of Peter Pan

Take to the water on the **Serpentine**, the snake-shaped stretch of water in the middle of the park. Rent a rowboat, swim in the lido, sunbathe, or feed the birds!

IT'S GOING TO GET WORSE

TREASURE HUNT

❶ Whose gold-encrusted memorial is opposite the Royal Albert Hall?

❷ Who used to live in Apsley House?

Don't want to grow up? Then join Peter Pan in **Kensington Gardens**. You'll find him playing his pipes to the fairies, squirrels, birds, and mice that scamper around him.

Feel like a good argument? Then join the orators and eccentrics who stand on their soapboxes at **Speakers' Corner** every Sunday. By law, anyone can speak here – but anyone can heckle as well!

The statue was erected in 1912.

🚇 Marble Arch, Hyde Park Corner, Lancaster Gate, Queensway, Knightsbridge

The most famous
princess in the world –
Diana, Princess of Wales
– lived in **Kensington
Palace** before her death
in 1997. People still leave
flowers in her memory.

Sights at a glance

1. Kensington Palace
2. Round Pond
3. Bandstand
4. Albert Memorial
5. Serpentine Gallery
6. Peter Pan
7. Fountains
8. Lido & Café
9. Horse Riding/ Rotten Row
10. Café
11. Boathouse
12. Bandstand
13. Apsley House
14. Speakers' Corner
15. Marble Arch

There are lots of activities available in the
park. You can cycle or inline skate on the specially
marked tracks, go horseback riding along **Rotten
Row**, watch the model boats on the Round
Pond, play tennis, or simply kick a ball
around with some friends.

🕐 5 am – Midnight 💷 Free

Tussaud's & Baker Street

GET YOUR PHOTO TAKEN with Arnold Schwarzenegger, stand between Mel Gibson and Brad Pitt, meet Saddam Hussein and all six wives of Henry VIII, play with the Beatles – in fact, get star-struck big time at Madame Tussaud's waxworks. It's grand, great, and in places very gory.

Planetarium

Tussaud's

Join the line for Madame Tussaud's next to Baker Street tube, and hours later you will emerge from the London Planetarium – the two buildings are joined together inside.

Sculptor uses photos for reference.

More than 150 measurements of the subject have to be taken before a waxwork is sculpted. The process takes six months and costs about $33,000. Each hair on the head is inserted individually, and finished models have their hair washed and styled regularly, just like a real person!

Pop star Kylie Minogue poses with her waxwork.

Eye color is matched exactly.

MAKING A WAXWORK

Put your head in a guillotine, burn at the stake, and still come out alive from the Chamber of Horrors, the cruelest place in London. Be sure to get out before they lock up for the night!

Madame Tussaud's ✉ Baker Street NW1 ☎ (020) 7935-6861
⊖ Baker Street ⊙ 10 am – 5:30 pm Mon – Fri (opens 9:30 am Sat, Sun)

Get lost in space at the **London Planetarium**, London's very own space observatory. Explore the solar system through touch-screen computers, and journey through the stars into (and back out of) a black hole with the spectacular Planetary Quest virtual reality show.

See a replica of Sherlock Holmes's study at the museum in Baker Street.

DID YOU KNOW?

★ Madame Tussaud learned her art in the 1770s from a doctor who made wax anatomical figures.

★ During the French Revolution, she made death masks of nobles who were guillotined, including King Louis XVI and Queen Marie Antoinette.

Elementary, my dear Watson!

One of the most famous addresses in London is **221b Baker Street**, home of the fictional detective Sherlock Holmes. You won't solve any crimes here – it never existed. But a museum recreating Holmes's rooms can be found between 237 and 239, and the dog barking in the background might be a Baskerville Hound!

Get on the case with the world's most famous fictional detective.

SHERLOCK HOLMES
CONSULTING DETECTIVE
221b Baker Street

TREASURE HUNT

❶ When did Sherlock Holmes live at 221b Baker Street?

❷ How much do you weigh on Jupiter?

❸ Whose statue stands outside Baker Street tube?

💲 Charge **www.** madame-tussauds.co.uk Sherlock Holmes Museum
☎ (020) 7935-8866 🕓 9:30 am – 6 pm 💲 Charge

London Zoo

ARE THERE LIONS in London? Tigers in the park? See for yourself at the London Zoo, home to animals from all round the world. There are over 12,000 creatures here – too many to see in one visit. You can even handle some animals – and talk to them, too. Visit the birdhouses, and some might answer you back!

Regent's Park surrounds the zoo, and a canal runs right past the famous aviary. Walk along the towpath, or even come by boat.

Llamas come from the Andes mountains in South America but are quite happy to pull you around the zoo in a cart. You can also **ride on a pony** or sit astride a camel.

Its a hard li

DID YOU KNOW?

★ London Zoo has a large conservation center at Whipsnade Wild Animal Park, in the countryside north of London. Among the rare creatures on display are Siberian tigers and one-horned Nepalese rhinos.

★ Many of the zoo's earliest inhabitants walked here from London Docks. In 1838, one of the giraffes panicked on Commercial Road when it saw a cow.

Only 300 Asiatic lions are left in the wild in India. Luckily, a large family thrives in London Zoo – ten cubs have been born since 1993. Stand behind the glass right next to the lioness as she plays with her cubs.

✉ Regent's Park, NW1 ☎ (020) 7722-3333
Ⓔ Camden Town 🕐 10 am – 4 pm daily

Conserving rare species is an important part of the zoo's work. Many animals face extinction in their natural habitat, but the zoo can protect them and breed new generations to expand their numbers. Some of the zoo-born animals are even returned to the wild to start their own families.

GOLDEN LION TAMARIN

Raw fish for everyone! Turn up at the right time, and you can see the animals fed by their keepers. **Penguins are fed** every day, snakes every week, but be careful in the Aquarium when the piranhas get hungry!

TREASURE HUNT

1. Who was Arfur?
2. What are jumbo scales?
3. What is a pudu?
4. What is another name for arachnophobia?

Become a tiger or a butterfly, a leopard or a giraffe, by getting your face painted next to the Clock Tower.

eing King of the Jungle

COOL FOR KIDS

★ Adopt an animal and have your name displayed in the zoo.

★ Watch lemurs, parrots, owls, rats, and other animals fly, leap, climb, hunt, and often misbehave in the Amphitheatre.

Charge
www. londonzoo.co.uk

Natural History Museum

The Museum is one of London's most famous landmarks. It's also covered in **animal carvings**, inside and out. Why not see how many you can find?

THE GIGANTIC DOORMAN at the Natural History Museum is *Diplodocus*, 86 ft (26 m) from nose to tail. A giant scorpion lurks round the corner, and there's a car half-buried by a fiery volcano. They even have a dodo, and dinosaur babies hatching out of their eggs – it's life as you've never seen it before!

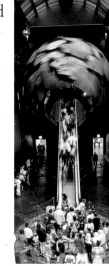

Volcanoes erupt, lightning strikes, and hurricanes blow in the **Earth Galleries**. All of the world's rare minerals and gemstones are here, and there's even a lump of moon rock!

Tree was finally cut down in 1892.

Leaf factory shows how plants make energy.

Shrink to 8/1,000th of your normal size and look **inside a leaf**, where you can see how plants get energy from the Sun and give the rest of us oxygen to breathe.

Plot the history of the world by counting tree rings in the great **Sequoia trunk**. The tree was born in 557AD, and added a ring of growth to its trunk every year, until it was 13 ft (4m) across and 260 ft (80m) high – taller than the museum!

✉ Cromwell Road SW7 ☎ (020) 7938-9123
Ө South Kensington

Beware of the Tyrannosaurus Rex!

Teeth up to 7 in (18 cm) long

TREASURE HUNT

❶ Where does an earthquake take place every few minutes?

❷ What are the only living creatures in the museum (apart from the curators)?

DID YOU KNOW?

★ The museum contains more than 68 million natural history specimens – most of them aren't on public display.

★ A 500-ft (150-m) deep well was drilled under the museum to tap into a supply of fresh water.

Don't stand too close to *Tyrannosaurus rex*: He's so big that he could chop you in half with one bite. Just as fearsome are the three *Deinonychus*, feasting on a dying *Tenontosaurus*. Not for the faint-hearted!

Whale skeletons

Blue whale model

Gasp at the sheer size of the Blue Whale, the largest creature ever to exist! Other mammals in the **Whale Hall** include dolphins, porpoises, and the extinct woolly mammoth, nearly the size of a red double-decker bus.

🕙 Mon – Sat 10 am – 5:50 pm, Sun 11 am – 5:50 pm
💷 Charge, kids free **www.** nhm.ac.uk

Science Museum

STEAM TRAINS AND JET ENGINES, biplanes and rockets, old clocks and nuclear reactors – all these and more are at the Science Museum. It can all be a bit confusing, but there are lots of green-shirted explainers on hand to make sense of everything!

AUTOGIRO FROM 1932

Before electricity, factories were powered by steam engines. Pressure from the boiling steam drives the pistons that turn the wheel. Noisy, powerful, and incredibly impressive!

DID YOU KNOW?

★ Charles Babbage's computer, designed between 1847–49, was so advanced that it wasn't built until 1991!

★ The first plane to fly across the Atlantic crashed-landed in a bog in Ireland at the end of its flight in 1919.

Science theory can be baffling, but science fact is great fun in the **Launch Pad**, where 50 interactive exhibits can be pulled, pushed, and played with, all in the cause of science – go on, you know you want to!

✉ Exhibition Road, SW7 ☎ (020) 7938-8000
⊖ South Kensington ⊕ 10 am – 6 pm daily

Yes, that battered-looking metal cone really did carry three astronauts to the Moon and back. It's the command module of Apollo 10, sitting next to a replica of a lunar lander. And they both look so small!

Dozens of aircraft, including the first to cross the Atlantic, hang in the museum. From fragile biplanes to powerful jets, and hot air balloons to helicopters, you can see the whole history of flight.

Take a half-million-mile trip to Kensington!

COOL FOR KIDS

★ Go in the flight simulator and learn to fly a plane.

★ Watch the Earth rotate under Foucault's swinging pendulum.

★ Drive, and crash, a car for real in the driving simulator.

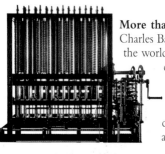

More than 150 years ago, Charles Babbage designed the world's first computer, capable of doing sums up to 31 digits long. A little like a pocket calculator, only for a bigger pocket!

Ever wanted to be a radio DJ? Then head for the **On Air Studio** and compile your own five-minute radio broadcast. Who knows, you could end up a star!

Work the mixing desk or stand behind the mike.

South Bank

HEAD OVER THE THAMES to the South Bank, the cultural heart of London, for great music, plays, movies, and art. Even if you're not paying to see an event, hang out here to browse in the bookstores, to visit the free exhibitions, or to have a drink in one of the many cafés.

South Bank Center

Plays in the National Theatre, music in the Queen Elizabeth and Festival halls, art at the Hayward Gallery, movies in the National Film Theatre – the South Bank is London's artistic center. There are often jugglers and other street entertainers by the riverbank, and regular free concerts happen in the foyer of the Festival Hall.

COOL FOR KIDS

★ You've seen the FA Hall of Fame, now get tickets to see a real soccer match at one the capital's many football stadiums.

★ Stroll along the riverbank or just sit and watch the world go by on the river.

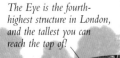

Music, movies, socce

The Eye turns 6,000 times a year.

The Eye is the fourth-highest structure in London, and the tallest you can reach the top of!

The London Eye is the largest observation wheel in the world – it's 434 ft (132.5 m) tall and weighs 15,000 tons. Get in one of its 32 capsules, and for 30 minutes you will have the view of a lifetime over London and the surrounding countryside. From the top, you can see 7 counties, 3 airports, 13 soccer league stadiums, and 36 Thames bridges!

DID YOU KNOW?

★ The Royal Festival Hall was built to celebrate the 1951 Festival of Britain – it was the Millennium Dome of its day!

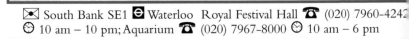

✉ South Bank SE1 ⊖ Waterloo Royal Festival Hall ☎ (020) 7960-4242
🕙 10 am – 10 pm; Aquarium ☎ (020) 7967-8000 🕙 10 am – 6 pm

Stroke a (non-sting) ray, catch a crab, and handle a starfish – all in the **London Aquarium**, home to fish and sea life from around the world. Look closely at the piranhas – some are vegetarian, but some would prefer a more meaty meal!

These sand tiger sharks don't eat people, but feed on smaller fish.

Many of the fish in the aquarium are pretty, but some are poisonous too!

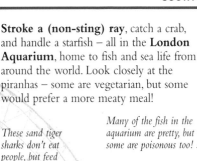

Jaws is alive and well and living in the London Aquarium! In fact, although they look fierce, the brown, sand tiger, and nurse sharks that stalk the tanks only eat other fish. But it's still not the place for a swim!

...harks, and the best views in London

The soccer players fans love to applaud, and the ones fans love to boo, are all in the Football Association's **FA Premier League** Hall of Fame – a fabulous celebration of the beautiful game. Stand next to the heroes of English soccer past and present and cheer them on!

London used to be governed from County Hall. Today it's home to the London Aquarium and the FA Hall of Fame.

GOALKEEPER'S GLOVES

ⓔ Charge; FA Hall of Fame ☎ (020) 7928-1800 ☽ 10 am – 6 pm
ⓔ Charge; London Eye **www.** ba-londoneye.com

Along the river

A RIVER TRIP is the best way to see the center of London, and you don't even have to walk! Most boats go downstream past the City to Greenwich and out to the Thames Barrier. Take a notebook or camera, as there is lots to record along the route.

Take a river boat from Charing Cross or Westminster piers – from here you can go downstream to Greenwich or upstream to Hampton Court. Some boats have guides who talk about famous sights along the banks, while others are simply river taxis.

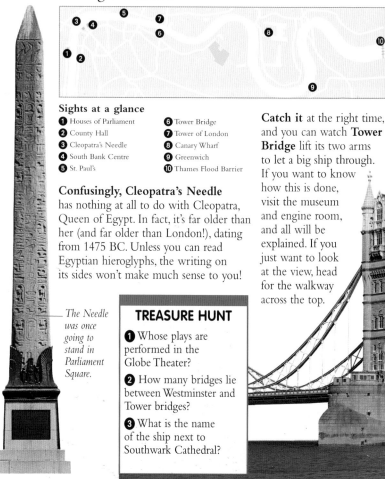

Sights at a glance

1. Houses of Parliament
2. County Hall
3. Cleopatra's Needle
4. South Bank Centre
5. St. Paul's
6. Tower Bridge
7. Tower of London
8. Canary Wharf
9. Greenwich
10. Thames Flood Barrier

Confusingly, Cleopatra's Needle has nothing at all to do with Cleopatra, Queen of Egypt. In fact, it's far older than her (and far older than London!), dating from 1475 BC. Unless you can read Egyptian hieroglyphs, the writing on its sides won't make much sense to you!

The Needle was once going to stand in Parliament Square.

Catch it at the right time, and you can watch **Tower Bridge** lift its two arms to let a big ship through. If you want to know how this is done, visit the museum and engine room, and all will be explained. If you just want to look at the view, head for the walkway across the top.

TREASURE HUNT

1. Whose plays are performed in the Globe Theater?

2. How many bridges lie between Westminster and Tower bridges?

3. What is the name of the ship next to Southwark Cathedral?

✉ River Trips from: Westminster Pier SW1, Charing Cross Pier WC2 (also Temple Pier WC2, Tower Pier EC3)

London has flooded several times in its long history, but there's no danger of it ever happening again, as the **Thames Barrier** rises up across the river to stop the flood tide from rushing in. It's one of the engineering wonders of the world, and strangely beautiful, too. If you break your trip here before returning, you can look around the visitor center to see how it all works.

DID YOU KNOW?

★ Canary Wharf originally handled ships full of bananas from the Canary Islands.

★ London's government used to operate from County Hall, opposite Parliament.

★ London Bridge used to have shops across it on either side. The current bridge was built without shops in 1972.

It's the tallest building in London, the second tallest in Europe, and has a flashing light on top to warn away airplanes. Unfortunately you can't get up the tower at **Canary Wharf** to admire the scenery!

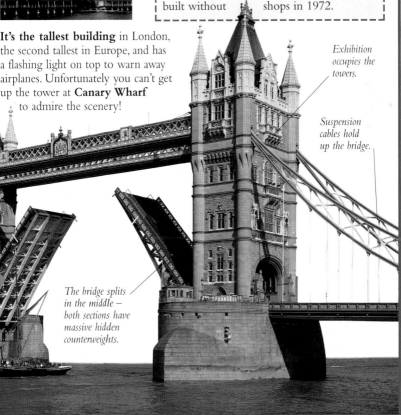

Exhibition occupies the towers.

Suspension cables hold up the bridge.

The bridge splits in the middle – both sections have massive hidden counterweights.

🚇 Westminster, Embankment, Charing Cross, Temple, Tower Hill
🕐 Mid-morning – evening 💷 Charge

The City & St. Paul's

THE CITY IS THE OLDEST part of London, and it is filled with narrow winding alleys, historic churches, and other buildings. Today, the City is also the financial capital of Europe. During the day it's packed with office workers, but during evenings and weekends, it's deserted – only 5,000 people actually live here.

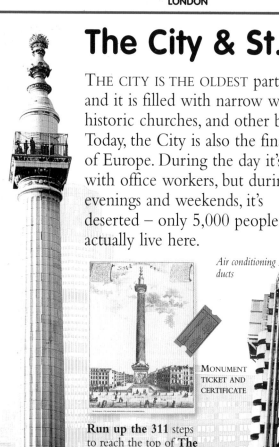

Air conditioning ducts

MONUMENT TICKET AND CERTIFICATE

Run up the 311 steps to reach the top of **The Monument**. It was built to commemorate the Great Fire of London, which started in nearby Pudding Lane, and destroyed most of the city in 1666. The view is great, and you get a certificate to prove you climbed it!

This collection of vast stainless steel pipes, acres of plate glass, and outsized heating ducts is actually the headquarters of **Lloyd's of London**, the largest insurance company in the world. You can't get inside, but the building looks fabulous from the outside, particularly when it is floodlit at night.

DID YOU KNOW?

★ The City of London is only one square mile in size and is separate from the rest of London, with its own Lord Mayor and police force.

★ In 1855 Britain's first public lavatory (for men only) was built in the forecourt of the Royal Exchange, in the City of London. The charge was one penny.

In a high-security vault under the Bank of England is all the gold owned by the British government. It's worth over £4.1 billion and, no, you can't help yourself! But you can touch a gold bar in the Bank's museum, and play on a virtual international currency exchange.

BANK OF ENGLAND SOUVENIRS

The Great Fire destroyed many London churches, including the medieval **St. Paul's Cathedral**. Christopher Wren designed its replacement, which was finished in 1708. Down in the crypt, you can see a model of Wren's original design, which is quite different from the finished building.

Climb up inside St. Paul's dome – and look down if you dare! If you talk in the **Whispering Gallery**, don't be surprised if people on the other side of the gallery – 100 ft (30 m) away – join in your conversation, as even the quietest whisper can be heard clearly by everyone – no secrets here!

The Cathedral actually has three domes, nested inside each other.

COOL FOR KIDS

★ Climb the 521 stairs to the top of St. Paul's – see if you can spot Wren's house across the river.

★ See barristers and judges come and go at the Old Bailey, England's central criminal court.

Museum of London

FROM AN IMPERIAL ROMAN outpost to the center of the British Empire and now a modern, international city, London has a long and colorful history. You can see it all in the Museum of London, where objects and photographs tell the story of this great city.

Sign from the Bull and Mouth Inn.

Soon after the Romans founded Londinium in AD43, they began to surround the city with a strong **stone wall** to keep out restless locals. You can still see traces of the wall near the museum and on Tower Hill.

Learn the

In medieval times, London's population was only about 50,000, but it was still the biggest city in England. People came from all over Europe to buy and sell goods, and quenched their thirst in the many inns or taverns.

TREASURE HUNT

❶ Whose diaries recorded the Great Fire as it happened?

❷ When was the Great Plague?

❸ Which famous poet lived in London during the 1300s?

On the second Friday of every November a new Lord Mayor of London is sworn into office in a ceremony dating back to 1215. The next day, the mayor rides through the City in an ornate gold coach, accompanied by bands, decorated floats, and military guards. Get there early to watch the fabulous **Lord Mayor's Show**!

The Great Fire of London broke out in Pudding Lane on September 2, 1666, and blazed for four days before burning itself out. Eighty percent of the city was destroyed, including 87 churches and 13,200 homes, but only nine people died.

See a recreation of the fire at the museum.

✉ London Wall EC2 ☎ (020) 7814-5601 ⊖ Barbican, St. Paul's
🕐 10 am – 5:50 pm Monday – Saturday, 12 pm – 5:50 pm Sunday

The museum has lots of exhibits especially interesting to kids.

Punch and Judy first appeared in London in 1662.

On building sites, even archaeologists have to wear hard hats!

JUDY

PUNCH

Over the centuries, generations of Londoners have left many things behind them. Today, if you peer through the fences around any building site, you may see archaeologists uncovering walls of long-forgotten buildings, old coins, pottery, and even the odd skeleton.

tory of London through the ages!

When not in use, the Lord Mayor's Coach is kept at the museum.

The coach was built in 1757.

DID YOU KNOW?

★ The Great Fire began at Pudding Lane and ended at Pie Corner!

★ The Thames used to freeze over during harsh winters, allowing Londoners to hold "frost fairs" on the ice.

£ Charge
www. museumoflondon.org.uk

London ships

THE RIVERBANKS OF LONDON are crammed with historic and interesting ships – until the 1960s, London was a thriving port. Some of the ships are museums, others floating cafés and restaurants. Leave the shore behind and experience life on the ocean waves, or as close as you can get on the River Thames!

TREASURE HUNT

❶ What is the name of the small yacht next to the *Cutty Sark*?

❷ What flag did pirates fly on their ships?

❸ Who was the first Englishman to sail round the world?

Walk the plank with pirates, then go into battle on

The Cutty Sark *carried tea from China to Europe.*

Down in Greenwich the *Cutty Sark* lords it over the town. In 1871 she took 107 days to sail from London to China, a world record at the time! Wander around the ship, and don't miss the collection of colorful figureheads on display in the lower hold.

St. Katharine Docks used to be packed with warehouses storing imported luxuries such as ivory and marble. Today, they're full of expensive apartments, historic boats, and luxury yachts from all around the world. It's still the closest you can get to a glimpse of what London's docks were like.

HMS *Belfast* ✉ Tooley St. SE1 ☎ (020) 7940-6328 ⊖ London Bridge ⊕ 10 am – 6 pm (5 pm Nov – Mar) *Cutty Sark* ✉ Greenwich SE10

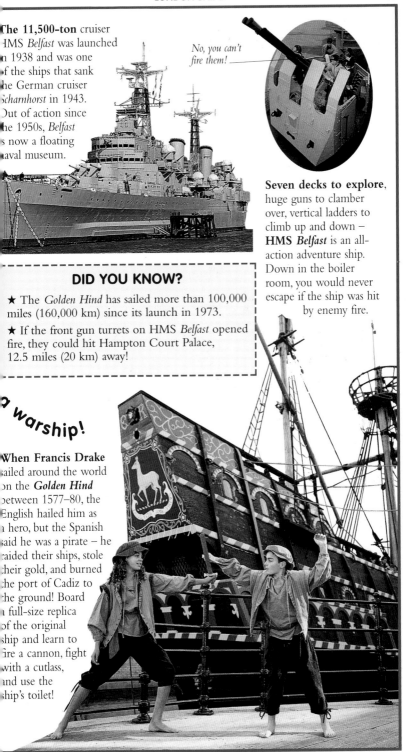

The **11,500-ton** cruiser HMS *Belfast* was launched in 1938 and was one of the ships that sank the German cruiser *Scharnhorst* in 1943. Out of action since the 1950s, *Belfast* is now a floating naval museum.

No, you can't fire them!

Seven decks to explore, huge guns to clamber over, vertical ladders to climb up and down – **HMS** *Belfast* is an all-action adventure ship. Down in the boiler room, you would never escape if the ship was hit by enemy fire.

DID YOU KNOW?

★ The *Golden Hind* has sailed more than 100,000 miles (160,000 km) since its launch in 1973.

★ If the front gun turrets on HMS *Belfast* opened fire, they could hit Hampton Court Palace, 12.5 miles (20 km) away!

a warship!

When Francis Drake sailed around the world on the **Golden Hind** between 1577–80, the English hailed him as a hero, but the Spanish said he was a pirate – he raided their ships, stole their gold, and burned the port of Cadiz to the ground! Board a full-size replica of the original ship and learn to fire a cannon, fight with a cutlass, and use the ship's toilet!

☎ (020) 8858-3445 🚉 Greenwich, Maze Hill *Golden Hind* ✉ Clink St. SE1 ☎ (020) 7403-0123 ⊖ London Bridge, Southwark

Tower of London

THE TOWER OF LONDON is an ancient royal prison dating back nearly 1,000 years. Lots of famous people from history were imprisoned and even executed here. Enjoy the most historic site in London – but make sure you get out safely!

TOWER OF LONDON SOUVENIRS

Legend has it that England will never be conquered while there are **ravens** at the tower. To make sure that that never happens, the birds' wings are clipped so that they can't fly! When the ravens die, they are buried in the moat:

The Beefeaters, or Yeoman Warders, are the Tower's guides and guards (Beefeater was once a term of abuse for an overfed servant!). On special occasions they wear a 16th-century red and gold uniform, but most days they turn out in dark blue.

TREASURE HUNT

❶ Which two wives of Henry VIII were executed on Tower Green?

❷ Why was the White Tower white?

❸ Who was the last prisoner held in the Queen's House?

✉ Tower Hill, EC3   ⊖ Tower Hill   ☎ (020) 7709-0765
🕒 9 am – 5 pm Tues – Sat (opens 10 am Sun, Mon, closes 4 pm in winter)

Most prisoners at the Tower arrived by river through **Traitors' Gate**. Many were hanged, drawn, and quartered (disemboweled and chopped up). The lucky ones just lost their heads!

he **Princes** in the ower were Edward V d his brother Richard. hey were placed here by eir uncle, Richard III, 1483, and were never en again...

ST. EDWARD'S CROWN

The Crown Jewels are the regalia used for royal coronations and state occasions. They drip with diamonds and other rare stones. Don't ask how much they are worth – they're priceless – and don't even think about stealing them!

The White Tower is the earliest surviving building.

There has been a fortress on Tower Hill since 1066, when **William the Conqueror** built a timber-and-earth castle here. Over the years, the Tower grew rapidly, serving as a palace, an arms factory, a royal mint, a zoo, a strongroom for the royal jewels, and, of course, a prison.

DID YOU KNOW?

★ Elizabeth I was imprisoned here by her sister Queen Mary for supposedly plotting against her.

★ At 9:53 pm every evening, the Beefeaters stage the Ceremony of the Keys to lock the gates of the Tower. By 10:00 pm, the Tower is secure for the night.

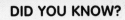

Greenwich

THE HOME OF TIME – the place where all the clocks in the world are set, and all the maps in the world are centered – Greenwich is in the middle of *everything*. Get there by boat and see the sights from the river. From the hill in Greenwich Park, the view across London is even better.

For more than two centuries the king's Astronomer Royal looked up at the stars from the observatory on top of the hill. The **Royal Observatory** staff have now moved to Cambridge, but they left lots of telescopes and other instruments behind for you to look at.

COOL FOR KIDS

★ Walk under the Thames to Docklands through the tunnel.

★ Have a picnic in Greenwich Park.

★ Go bargain-hunting at the market.

★ Fly a kite in the park or on next-door Blackheath.

Set your watch at the home of

Clocks all over the world are set by Greenwich Mean Time, the international measure of time since 1884. To make sure no-one in Greenwich ever forgets what time it is, there's this strange 24-hour clock on the observatory wall!

Stand one side of this line, and you are in the eastern half of the world. Stand on the other, and you've moved to the west. This is the **Greenwich Meridian**, which divides the world in two. Look at a map of the world, and the 0° line passes straight through Greenwich.

A brass strip marking the meridian runs through the park

Sights at a glance

❶ Foot Tunnel
❷ *Gipsy Moth IV*
❸ *Cutty Sark*
❹ Greenwich Pier
❺ Royal Naval College
❻ Queen's House
❼ National Maritime Museum
❽ Greenwich Park
❾ Old Royal Observatory

✉ Greenwich SE10 🚇 Greenwich, Maze Hill
Observatory and National Maritime Museum ☎ (020) 8858-4422

The National Maritime Museum is no place for landlubbers – it's devoted to Britain's seafaring past. Rig a sailing ship, send messages with signal flags, and hear tales of daring explorers and naval commanders. Get your sea legs ready and prepare to set sail!

The museum also has exhibits about exploring under the sea – like this old diver's helmet!

...time, then stand on both sides of the world at once!

Nelson was a hero before Trafalgar and had lots of medals.

Huge anchors like this needed teams of sailors to pull them up from the seabed.

Anchors Aweigh! Greenwich is full of reminders of the sea, from massive anchors outside the Maritime Museum to ships such as the huge *Cutty Sark* and the tiny *Gipsy Moth IV*.

On October 21, 1805, the British fleet, led by Admiral Nelson, defeated the French in the famous Battle of Trafalgar off the coast of Spain. But Nelson, Britain's greatest naval hero, was killed by a French musket shot. The museum has Nelson's uniform on display, complete with bullet hole!

NELSON'S UNIFORM

TREASURE HUNT

❶ Why did the Astronomer Royal leave Greenwich?

❷ Why does the ball drop down its rod on the roof of the Royal Observatory?

❸ Why is the Naval College split in half?

This huge anchor is from Queen Victoria's royal yacht, Britannia.

🕘 Museum and Observatory 10 am – 5 pm daily

💷 Charge – combined ticket **WWW.** nmm.ac.uk

Millennium Dome

DOME FROM SPACE

IT'S BIG, IT'S IMPRESSIVE, and it's built to celebrate an event that only happens once in a thousand years. There is no other building like it in the world, which is just one good reason to go and visit. What's more, the Dome is only open for a year, so get there quick and enjoy it while it lasts!

COVERING THE DOME

The Dome is made up of 970,000 square feet (970,000 sq m) of woven glass fiber, stronger than steel and coated with Teflon to keep out the rain. The panels are held up by over 44 miles (72 km) of steel cable, attached to **twelve towering masts**. The materials used in the Dome are made to be environmentally friendly, and to make it completely "green," rainwater from the roof is recycled into the toilets!

Inside the Dome, fourteen zones explore the mind, body, environment, and almost everything else. Each zone uses the latest technology to create interactive exhibits. There's also a huge central arena the size of Trafalgar Square where live shows take place, and a vast movie theater next door.

Come to the Dome for

Dome fabric is made of 144 separate sections.

✉ Greenwich SE10 ☎ (0870) 606-2000 ⊖ North Greenwich
⊙ 10 am – 6 pm (later openings in summer)

Next time you are up in space, look down on East London. The Dome will be clearly visible through the cockpit window!

The Dome

Greenwich

With acrobats, spectacular visual effects, and a rocking soundtrack, the **Millennium Show** tells the story of a dreamy boy and an go-getting girl as their world is turned upside down by events.

The riverbank near the Dome has been transformed into an ideal habitat for a variety of animals, ranging from shrimp and fish to birds like oystercatchers and herons.

DID YOU KNOW?

★ If you and 2,499 of your friends joined hands, you could form a chain right around the base of the Dome.

★ Alternatively, turn up with 94 African elephants and line them up across the floor. They would just about touch both sides!

the experience of a thousand years!

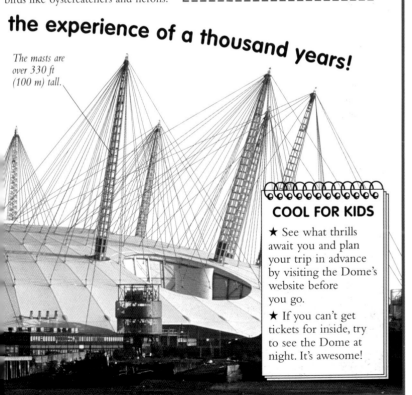

The masts are over 330 ft (100 m) tall.

COOL FOR KIDS

★ See what thrills await you and plan your trip in advance by visiting the Dome's website before you go.

★ If you can't get tickets for inside, try to see the Dome at night. It's awesome!

£ Charge

www. dome2000.co.uk; www.greenwich2000.co.uk

Just for kids

LONDON HAS SEVERAL PLACES just for kids, and adults who still want to be kids. London's toy museums have threadbare teddies, huge train sets, dolls old and new, toys from spinning tops to computer games, and all the things you thought you grew out of years ago. Who knows, you might even be able to shout "I've got one of those!"

The Museum of Childhood in Bethnal Green is always full of kids – with ages from 4 to 84! For the smaller ones, there are lots of toys you can actually play with.

With everything from rocking horses to flapper dolls, Star Wars™ toys to old comics, racing cars to giant Lego blocks, the Museum of Childhood and Pollock's Toy Museum are full of all those toys you most wanted but never got from Santa Claus.

MUSEUM OF CHILDHOOD SOUVENIRS

Antique rocking horses were made of wood and plaster.

TREASURE HUNT

❶ When did Barbie first make her appearance?

❷ Where will you find a Phenakistoscope and a Heliocinegraphe?

Museum of Childhood ✉ Cambridge Heath Rd. E2 ☎ (020) 8983-520● ⊖ Bethnal Green ⊙ 10 am – 5:50 pm (2 pm - 5:50 pm Sun, closed Fri)

COOL FOR KIDS

★ Once a year – usually the first Friday in August – take your teddy bear to the teddy bear's picnic in Battersea Park.

★ Take a trip to one of London's many children's zoos or city farms.

Thousands of dolls hang out in the Museum of Childhood - from antique wooden and china ones right through to Barbie and Ken. There's also a huge collection of their houses to see here, too. You can't play with most of them, but you can look, and wish they belonged to you.

Toys for boys, and lots of them, at Bethnal Green, with model trains and cars, **toy soldiers** and their forts, and modern action figures. Check out the doll displays, too, for Action Man and other boys' dolls.

Some toy trains are just to look at – others are set up on tracks so you can watch them in action.

Back in the 1800s, Benjamin Pollock made toy theaters and sold theater kits with the slogan "a penny plain, two pence colored." The actors were little paper figures on the ends of sticks. You can see these fabulous **miniature theaters** in Pollock's Toy Museum, and even buy replicas to take home and make yourself!

Pollock's Toy Museum is also full of toys, puppets, and other fun stuff. Meet Eric the teddy bear, who was born in 1905, an Egyptian clay mouse who is 4,000 years old, and famous folk like Punch and Judy.

(£) Free; Pollock's Toy Museum ✉ Scala St. W1 ☎ (020) 7636-3452
(E) Goodge St. ⊙ 10 am – 5 pm Mon – Sat (£) Charge

Horrible London

MURDER, MAYHEM, BLOOD, and gore are as much a part of London as Buckingham Palace or a red double-decker bus. The city may be more peaceful now, but you can relive its violent past in dungeons, prisons, and many other blood-soaked places.

The Old Operating Theatre, Museum & Herb Garret.
Summer events & workshops for families & children.

Every Thursday
HELP THE MEDICINE GO DOWN!

22nd July, 12th & 26th August, 2.30pm.
Pills, Potions, Poisons.
Wierd and exotic remedies of the past, from the hands-on Herb Garret. Make your own silver pills to go, scratch 'n' sniff herbs and ointments. Discover the medicinal uses of roasted vipers and baths of sheep's heads. Is it magic, malady, or medicine?

29th July, 19th August, 2nd September, 2.30pm.
Victorian Surgery.
"I have broken my arm, I am a dead man!"
A demonstration of the ordeals of surgery without anaesthesia, when a patient's fate rested on the speed of the surgeon's knife.
A real amputation kit awaits! How will you survive?

The Old Operating Theatre, Museum and Herb Garret.

OPERATING ROOM PROGRAM

Misbehave a few centuries ago, and you would have been thrown into the Clink, a damp, cold prison for the debtors, heretics, criminals, and lowlife of South London. The prisoners may have gone, but the **Clink Prison Museum** is still full of reminders of life behind bars.

Heads on spikes on display in the London Dungeon

DID YOU KNOW?

★ The first head placed on London Bridge belonged to William Wallace, the Scottish freedom fighter executed in 1305. He is better known today as Braveheart, as played by Mel Gibson.

★ Both the Duke of Clarence, eldest son of King Edward VII, and the painter Walter Sickert have been suggested as the true identity of Jack the Ripper.

For centuries, the heads of traitors and other rebels were boiled, coated in tar, and stuck on poles on top of London Bridge. When the monarchy was restored after the English Civil War, the body of Oliver Cromwell, who had ordered the execution of King Charles I, was dug up and beheaded. The head was displayed here to set an example to traitors.

London Dungeon ✉ Tooley Street, SE1 ⊖ London Bridge
☎ (020) 7403-7221 ⏲ 10:30 am – 5 pm £ Charge

See how surgery was once performed in the old operating room of St. Thomas's Hospital. No painkillers or antibiotics here – just a wooden table where the patient was bound, gagged, and blindfolded, and sawdust on the floor to mop up the blood. Few survived an operation!

Jack the Ripper killed five women in London's East End in the fall of 1888. The Ripper was never caught, and his identity remains a mystery to this day. Take a guided walk from Tower Hill to the scenes of his crimes.

COOL FOR KIDS

★ Visit the House of Detention, a small basement prison in Clerkenwell.

★ Enter the Chamber of Horrors in Madame Tussaud's.

★ See the spot on Tower Hill where traitors were executed.

Explore the darker side of London's history!

Get scared out of your wits at the **London Dungeon**, the most frightening place in the world! Watch the Druids perform human sacrifice at Stonehenge, see Anne Boleyn beheaded, and join a roomful of people dying of the plague. If you survive all that, go on the River of Death boat ride to your own execution!

The Clink ✉ Clink Street, SE1 ⊖ London Bridge ☎ (020) 7403-6515
🕙 10 am – 6 pm ⓕ Charge

London markets

THE BEST PLACES TO SHOP in London are the street markets, which sell everything from rare records to secondhand clothes, fabulous jewelry to exotic foods. Join the bustle, keep your wits about you, and you might get yourself a bargain!

Get a pair of decent boots, then you'll be ready for more pavement-pounding!

COOL FOR KIDS

★ Get a taste of the Caribbean at Brixton market – reggae music, wooly hats, and fruits and vegetables you've probably never seen in your life!

★ Get your hair plaited at – well, almost anywhere!

Most of the big markets happen on the weekend, but some, like Covent Garden, are open all week. Portobello and Camden are usually the most crowded, so keep an eye on your money!

There's only one place to go for big boots, New Age ornaments, and records – **Camden** has the biggest, noisiest market in London. Don't take too much money with you – you might want to spend it all!

Camden has loads of different markets for clothes, furniture, and food.

Delicious Bengali sweets for sale in Brick Lane!

Bangladesh meets London at **Brick Lane**, home to the city's Bengali community. There are miles of colorful fabrics to buy, fabulous bhangra music to listen to, and fantastic food, from sweets to samosas, to eat!

Flowers, music, food,

Camden ⊖ Camden Town ⊙ Saturdays, Sundays
Portobello ⊖ Ladbroke Grove, Notting Hill Gate ⊙ Fridays, Saturdays

The longest market in London is Portobello Road, which stretches for over a mile. At the south end, there's an antique market. In the middle you can find fruits, vegetables, and new clothes, and at the north end is a busy secondhand clothes, jewelry, and record market. With only two directions to go, there's no chance of getting lost!

Portobello has more than 2,000 stalls selling antiques and collectibles.

DID YOU KNOW?

★ One of the first streets to be lit by electricity in London was Electric Avenue, the main street in Brixton market.

★ Brick Lane was the site of the brick kilns that helped rebuild London after the Great Fire of 1666.

Shop for crafts at Greenwich and Covent Garden markets – they're not cheap, but you can find some lovely gifts to take home. Greenwich is also good for old books, and Covent Garden has an antiques market on Mondays.

The prettiest market in London has to be **Columbia Road**. This is London's main flower market, and even if you don't buy anything, you can still enjoy the colors and smells!

Hangings for sale at Greenwich market

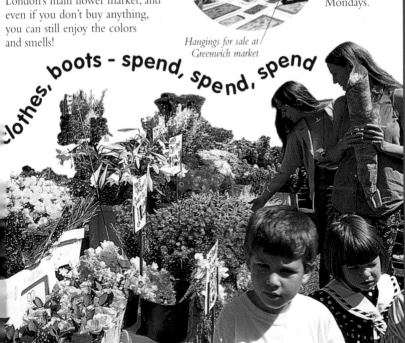

clothes, boots – spend, spend, spend

Brick Lane ⊖ Liverpool Street ☺ Sunday Mornings
Columbia Road ⊖ Liverpool Street ☺ Sunday mornings

London at war

AS BRITAIN'S CAPITAL, London is packed with reminders of war, from statues in the streets to museums of military equipment and wartime experiences. Mainland Britain hasn't been invaded for centuries, but bombs from the skies brought war home to many Londoners in the 1940s.

The Imperial War Museum is overflowing with military history and hardware, including the two *huge* guns outside, and this Polaris **nuclear missile** (it's not armed!) You can see exhibitions about codebreaking, military intelligence, and equipment from World War I through to the Gulf War and beyond.

Jet engine intakes

The RAF Museum in Hendon, North London, is home to some of the most famous military aircraft in the world. See just how small and flimsy a Spitfire fighter was, and learn how a Harrier Jump Jet manages to take off vertically.

Soldiers had to climb out of their trenches to advance.

Millions of British, French, American, and German soldiers lived and fought in muddy **trenches** for months on end during World War I (1914–18). Relive their horrible experiences at the Imperial War Museum, and be glad you'll never have to fight in a trench!

Imperial War Museum ✉ Lambeth Rd. SE1 ☎ (020) 7416-5000
🚇 Lambeth North 🕙 10 am – 6 pm 💷 Charge **www.** iwm.org.uk

During World War II (1939–45), Prime Minister Winston Churchill and his cabinet held meetings underground in the **Cabinet War Rooms**. Here they had a dining room, beds, and even a shooting range. You can see the hot-line telephone connecting Churchill to the US President, and maps of the world showing where the fighting was taking place.

Life was very different during World War II. The people of London were terrified of poisoned gas attacks. Everyone had to carry a gas mask with them, and the underground stations were turned into bomb shelters. Because Britain was cut off from Europe and America, almost everything had to be rationed.

CHILD'S GAS MASK AND HOLDER

Ration books entitled you to a weekly allowance of meat, sugar, and butter.

RATION BOOK

Nozzle swivels to direct exhaust downward and push the plane upward.

HARRIER JUMP JET

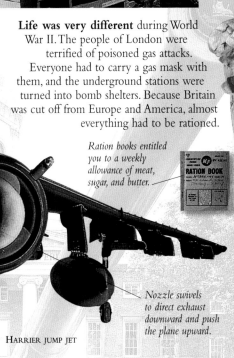

TREASURE HUNT

❶ Who was president of the USA during World War II?

❷ When was the Battle of Britain?

❸ Which famous sculptor sketched people in the Underground during the Blitz?

During the Blitz of 1940–41, London and other British cities were bombed almost every night. Thousands of people were killed, and many buildings destroyed. Learn what life was like during the Blitz in displays at the Imperial War Museum and the RAF Museum.

RAF Museum ✉ Hendon NW4 ☎ (0900) 1600-563 Ⓔ Colindale
Cabinet War Rooms ✉ SW1 ☎ (020) 7930-6961 Ⓔ Westminster

Day trips

JUST BECAUSE YOU'RE STAYING in London, you don't have to spend every day there. Take a short train or car journey out of the city, where there's lots of other things to do. Royal palaces, vast parks, scary roller coasters, and wild animals are all great ideas for a day out!

TREASURE HUNT

❶ What's special about the clock in Hampton Court's Clock Court?

❷ Where was Lego invented?

❸ What game is played indoors at Hampton Court?

Chessington used to be a zoo, and there are still some animals and birds to see. But the best animals are your fellow humans – watch them getting scared out of their wits on the roller coasters and other death-defying rides!

Ride the Rattlesnake roller coaster!

Hold on to your lunch – you can

Wild rides, Lego-brick cities, mystifying mazes,

Seastorm and Rameses' Revenge are wet and scary, the Vampire hangs in midair, and the Rattlesnake bites back. New ride on the block at Chessington is the Samurai "spin and spew"!

Chessington 🚉 South Chessington ☎ (01372) 727227
www. chessington.co.uk Legoland 🚉 Windsor ☎ (0990) 040404

Ride a Lego Intercity train to Lego Scotland, or take a Lego Eurostar to Lego France. Even better, ride the wet and wonderful Pirate Falls or the spooky Dragon! Join in the fun at **Legoland**, home of giant Lego models and miniature monuments.

DID YOU KNOW?

★ There were once four mazes at Hampton Court, and there are plans to restore the other three soon.

★ More than 1.6 million people visit Chessington every year, so there are often lines to get on the rides. Get there early for maximum fun!

The Hampton Court Maze is made of yew hedges.

Get lost! People have been wandering around Hampton Court **Maze** since 1714, when it was first laid out. Start at the beginning, walk toward the middle, and then realize you're lost. Help!

Learn swordplay from an English Civil War Cavalier.

istoric houses...

Hampton Court Palace has grown and grown since 1514. Get scared in the **Haunted Gallery**, slum it in the Tudor kitchens, and admire the magnificent royal apartments and gardens – it's all pretty posh!

www. legoland.co.uk Hampton Court 🚉 Hampton Court
☎ (020) 8781-9500 **www.** hrp.org.uk

Useful addresses

WHEN YOU'VE HAD ENOUGH of fighting the crowds at London's big attractions, you might want to go somewhere more relaxing, or grab something to eat!

PARKS, PLAYGROUNDS, & CITY FARMS

COVENT GARDEN AND BLOOMSBURY

Coram's Fields
✉ Guildford Street, WC1
(near British Museum)
☎ City Farm: (020) 7837-6138

Drury Lane Playground
✉ Drury Lane, WC2
(near Covent Garden)

PICCADILLY

Green Park
✉ Piccadilly SW1

St. James's Park
✉ The Mall SW1

Hyde Park
✉ Park Lane W1

CITY AND EAST LONDON

Mudchute Farm
✉ Pier Street, E14
(near Canary Wharf)
☎ (020) 7515-5901

Stepping Stones Farm
(City Farm)
✉ Stepney Way, E1
☎ (020) 7790-8204

Spitalfields Farm Association
(City Farm)
✉ Weaver Street, E1
☎ (020) 7247-8762

Victoria Park
✉ Hackney, E9

NORTH LONDON

Hayward Playground
✉ Islington N7

Hampstead Heath
✉ Hampstead NW3

Primrose Hill
✉ Camden NW1
(near London Zoo)

Paddington Street Playground
✉ Paddington St. NW1
(near Baker Street)

Queen's Park
✉ Kilburn NW6

Regent's Park
✉ Marylebone NW1
(near Baker Street, London Zoo)

SOUTH OF THE RIVER

Archbishop's Park
✉ Lambeth Road SE1
(near Imperial War Museum, Aquarium, London Eye)

Battersea Park
✉ Battersea SW11
☎ Children's Zoo: (020) 8871-7540

Blackheath
✉ Greenwich SE10

Brockwell Park
✉ Brixton SW2

Clapham Common
✉ Clapham SW4

Greenwich Park
✉ Rotherhithe SE11

Southwark Park
✉ Greenwich SE10

Vauxhall City Farm
✉ Tyers Street, SE11
☎ (020) 7582-4204

WEST LONDON

Kensington Gardens
✉ Kensington Gore W8

Holland Park
✉ Kensington High Street, Kensington W8

Chelsea Playground
✉ Royal Hospital Grounds, Chelsea SW3

PLACES TO EAT

COVENT GARDEN AND SOHO

Capital Café
✉ Charing Cross Road, Leicester Square WC1
☎ (020) 7484-8888

Chuen Cheng Ku
✉ 17 Wardour Street, Soho W1
☎ (020) 7437-1398

Luna Nuova
✉ 22 Shorts Gardens, Covent Garden WC2
☎ (020) 7836-4110

PJ's Grill
✉ 30 Wellington Street, Covent Garden WC2
☎ (020) 7240-7529

Rainforest Café
✉ Shaftesbury Avenue, Soho W1
☎ (020) 7434-3111

Rock Garden
✉ Covent Garden WC2
☎ (020) 7836-4052

Signor Zilli
✉ 41 Dean Street, Soho W1
☎ (020) 7734-3924

Smollensky's on the Strand
✉ 105 The Strand, Covent Garden WC2
☎ (020) 7497-2101

PICCADILLY

Hard Rock Café
✉ 150 Old Park Lane, Piccadilly W1
☎ (020) 7629-0382

Smollensky's Balloon
✉ 1 Dover Street, Piccadilly W1
☎ (020) 7491-1199

WEST LONDON

Chicago Rib Shack
✉ 1 Raphael Street, Knightsbridge SW7
☎ (020) 7581-5595

Geale's Fish Restaurant
✉ 2 Farmer Street, Kensington W8
☎ 020 7727-7969

Sticky Fingers
✉ 1A Phillimore Gardens, Kensington W8
☎ (020) 7938-5338

FURTHER AFIELD

The Boiled Egg and Soldier
✉ 63 Northcote Road, SW11
☎ (020) 7223-4894

Tootsie's
✉ Kew Road, Richmond
☎ 020 8948-4343

ndex

Acknowledgments

The author
Simon Adams studied at London University and has lived in the city ever since. He travels everywhere on buses and tubes, and sometimes uses his bike if he is feeling energetic. When he began writing this book, he thought he knew a lot about London, but like every tourist, the more places he visits, the more he wants to find out. Simon writes history and other nonfiction books for children, and spends his evenings in jazz clubs.

Dorling Kindersley would like to thank the following for their help in the production of this book: Maggie Crowley for editorial help, Olivia Triggs for design assistance, Sue Lightfoot for the index, Chris Orr Associates for the map artwork on the inside front cover, Stephen Oliver and Steve Gorton for additional photography, Natasha Trinnaman, Bradley Whitby, Emily and Kashi Gorton for modeling, and Marie Osborn for picture research assistance.

PICTURE CREDITS

The publishers would like to thank the following people for their kind permission to reproduce the following photographs:

Key: a = above; b = below; c = center; f = far; l = left; n = near; r = right; t = top

Every effort has been made to trace copyright holders and we apologize for any unintentional omissions. We will be pleased to add appropriate acknowledgements to any subsequent edition of this publication.

Special photography: Dave King, Mike Dunning, Roland Kemp, Matthew Ward

Ardea London Ltd: Ron & Valerie Taylor 37cl. **Sofia Ruiz Bartolini:** 50-51b. **BBC Experience:** 19tr. **Bridgeman Art Library, London / New York:** Rocking horse, English, 1840, Private Collection 52b; The Princes Edward and Richard in the Tower, 1878 (oil on canvas) by Sir John Everett Millais (1829-96), Royal Holloway and Bedford New College, Surrey, UK 47tl. **British Museum, London:** 22-23, 22l, 22r, 22t, 23c, 23b, 23t. **Britstock-ifa:** Roger Cracknell 13tl; Siebig 45t. **Cabaret Mechanical Theatre:** 16c. **Chessington World of Adventures:** 60-61, 60t. **Bruce Coleman Ltd:** Derek Croucher 24-25. © **Crown Copyright: Historic Royal Palaces 1999:** 61b. **E.T. Archive:** National Gallery London 15t. **The F. A. Premier League Hall of Fame:** 37b. **Robert Harding Picture Library:** 40l, 41tr, 41b, 44b, 48t; Adam Woolfitt 8cb; Adina Tovy 54cr; C. Bowman 12ctr; Louise Murray 54-55; N. Boyd 17bl; Nelly Boyd 56cr; Nigel Francis 6crb, 39t, 61t; Nik Wheeler 29c; Philip Craven 61c; Raj Kamal 5t; Vicky Skeet 10crb; Walter Rawlings

30t. **Hayes Davidson:** 16b. **HMS** *Belfast:* 45tr. **Imperial War Museum:** 8b, 59t. **The London Aquarium:** 37t. **The London Dungeon:** 56bl, 57br. **London Transport Museum:** 10clt; Richard Kalina 10t. **Madame Tussaud's, London:** 28c, 28bl, 28bc, 28br, 29t. **Museum Of London:** 42cl, 42-43, 42b, 43tl. **National Maritime Museum, London:** 48c, 49cr, 49t. **National Railway Museum, York:** 53c. **The Natural History Museum, London:** 32tr, 32cr, 32bl, 33bl, 33t. **Times Newspaper Limited:** 30-31. **Old Operating Theatre Museum and Herb Garret:** 56tr, 56-57. **PA News Photo Library:** Neil Munns 36-37. **Pollock's Toy Museum:** 53crb, 53b. © **QA Photos Ltd:** Jim Byrne 50tl. **Royal Air Force Museum, Hendon:** 59b. **Rex Features:** 3c, 5b, 10b, 20b, 20t, 24l, 46l, 47c, 52t; Andre Camara 7cla; Andrew Testa 40r; Edward Webb 55c; John Stephen 41ca; Kathryn Jones 25cl; PH Jorgensen 12tl; Tony Kyriacou 43tr. **The Royal Collection © 1999 Her Majesty Queen Elizabeth II:** John Freeman 25tr. **Nick Wood/David Marks/Julia Barfield Ltd:** 36c, 36b. **Science Museum:** 6cra, 6cr, 34cl, 34b, 35cb, 35b; Geoff Dann 6tr, 35tr. **Spot Image 1998:** 50-51tl. **Tony Stone Images:** Andrew Errington 54t; David Ball 55t; David H. Endersbee 6cla, 6cb, 38-39, 38t, 62-63; Ian Murphy 14b, 18; Janet Gill 2, 12-13; Joe Cornish 26tr, 58-59; John Lamb 6c, 39c; Michael Harris 32tl; Rex A. Butcher 19bl; Tim Brown 1, 15b; Tony Wiles 7cb. **Telegraph Colour Library:** A. J. Stirling 46-47; Francesca Yorke 7tr. **Unicorn Theatre:** Ivan Kyncl 21c.

Jacket: London Transport Museum: front tr, inside front tl. **Museum Of London:** back cra. **The Natural History Museum, London:** front cra. **Pictor International:** back tr. © **QA Photos Ltd.:** Jim Byrne front bc. **Rex Features:** Edward Webb inside front c; Nick Bailey front l.

Personal details

A JOURNAL IS A GREAT WAY to capture
memories of a wonderful visit to London.
Start your personal record here.

My Name ....

My Age ....

My Home Address ....

....

....

....

Arrival

I arrived in London on ....

at ....

The journey was ....

Hotel

I stayed at ....

My room number was ....

My visit lasted ....

Departure

I left London on ....

at ....

The journey was ....

I visited London with ....

....

....

London favorites

USE THESE PAGES to record your favorite
experiences on your trip to London.

What were the best
places you went to?

....
....
....
....
....
....

What was the tallest
building you went up
in London?

....
....
....

What could you
see from the top?

....
....
....
....
....
....
....

What was the single best thing you did in London?

....
....
....

What was the best souvenir you collected on your trip?
Where did you buy it?

....
....
....

London has a huge
variety of foods
available – list the
different things
you tried, and
whether you
liked them
or not!

Plenty of food for thought!

....
....
....
....
....
....
....

What was the best trip you took while in London?

....
....
....

Stick your favorite London photo here!

I-spy

WHEN YOU'RE OUT AND ABOUT in London, you can try these fun activities with your family.

Who will be the first to spot these London sights?

A police officer on the beat

Eros

A red telephone box

St. Paul's Cathedral

A guardsman

The tower at Canary Wharf

A London Underground sign

Collect these **souvenirs** and keep them in the pocket at the back of this book:

1 London Transport travelcard

2 Copper coins with the Queen's head

3 Postcard from a museum

4 Theater flyer

5 A first-class stamp

6 London Underground pocket map

7 Entrance tickets

Funtastic London facts

HERE ARE SOME interesting facts about London that you might not know!

★ The statue of Justice on top of the Old Bailey holds scales to weigh the evidence and a sword to deliver punishment. She wears a crown, but unlike some other Justices around the world, she's not blindfolded.

Justice is modeled on the Roman goddess Justica.

★ Around 7 million people currently live in Greater London (the city and its outer boroughs). That's 1.5 million fewer people than there were 60 years ago!

★ London buses have been running since 1829. The first underground trains ran in 1863, and were pulled by miniature steam engines!

★ The statue of a woman in a chariot next to Westminster tube station commemorates Boudicca, a British queen who burned Roman London to the ground in AD61.

★ The Strand, which runs from Trafalgar Square to the City, used to be the beach of the Thames River. Saxon traders ran their boats ashore here, and lived around Covent Garden.

★ The most famous Mayor of London, Dick Whittington from the fairy tale, really was Lord Mayor three times in the 1400s.

★ Marble Arch stands on the site of Tyburn gallows, where criminals used to be hanged!

London quick quiz

BY THE END OF YOUR VISIT you should be a London expert – test your knowledge here!

1 What's the clock tower at Parliament really called? ....
....

2 What color is the Circle Line?
....

3 What is Eros's real name?..........
....
....

4 Where can you step inside a leaf?...............
....
....
....

5 What kind of market was Covent Garden originally?...........................
....
....

6 What is the range of HMS *Belfast*'s guns?..............
....
....

7 What does Trooping the Color celebrate?..................
....
....

8 Where can you see Peter Pan and go boating?............
....

9 Where was Admiral Horatio Nelson killed?.......
....
....

10 How long does it take to make a Madame Tussaud's waxwork?..............
....
....

11 Where is London Zoo's wildlife park?..................
....
....

12 Which mission does the space capsule at the Science Museum come from? ....
....
....

19 When was the first Punch and Judy show in London?..............................
....
....

20 What's the proper name for a Beefeater?....................
....
....
....

13 Where is the Rosetta Stone?...............................
....
....

14 Where can you pick up cheap theater tickets?.........
....
....

15 What types of shark can you see at the London Aquarium?.......................
....
....

16 When was the current London Bridge built?
....

17 How much were Pollock's toy theater kits?...
....

18 Who built St. Paul's Cathedral?........................
....
....

Can you guess the height of London's Big Ben?

Answers

TREASURE HUNT

Page 13
1. Richard I, the Lionheart.
2. The Chancellor of the Exchequer.
3. 20th-century Christian Martyrs.

Page 15
1. Charles I, James II, and George IV.
2. Admiralty Arch.
3. In a lamppost next to South Africa House.
4. On the floor at their feet.

Page 18
1. The Greek God of Love
2. It's the name of a kind of stiff collar.
3. Aluminum

Page 23
1. The Rosetta Stone.
2. Bastet.
3. Chesspieces discovered on the Isle of Lewis.
4. Sir Hans Sloane, the Museum's founder.

Page 26
1. Prince Albert, Queen Victoria's husband.
2. The Duke of Wellington, who won the Battle of Waterloo.

Page 29
1. 1881–1904.
2. 2.5 times as much as on Earth.
3. Sherlock Holmes, of course!

Page 31
1. An Asian lion that used to live at the zoo.
2. Scales for weighing elephants!
3. The world's smallest deer.
4. Fear of spiders.

Page 33
1. In the Earth Galleries.
2. The ants in the Creepy-Crawlies display.

Page 38
1. William Shakespeare's. 2. Eight.

Page 42
1. Samuel Pepys' diaries.
2. 1665.
3. Geoffrey Chaucer

Page 44
1. *Gipsy Moth IV*, which Francis Chichester sailed around the world alone in 1966–67.
2. The skull-and-crossbones, or Jolly Roger.
3. Sir Francis Drake, in 1577–1580.

Page 46
1. Anne Boleyn and Catherine Howard.
2. The stone used to be regularly whitewashed.
3. Rudolph Hess, Adolph Hitler's deputy, who was imprisoned here 1941–45.

Page 49
1. The bright lights and pollution were stopping him from seeing the stars.
2. So that sailors and clockmakers could accurately set their timepieces.
3. So it doesn't spoil the view of the river from the Queen's House.

Page 52
1. 1959 – she was launched at the New York Toy Fair.
2. In Pollock's Toy Museum – they're both optical toys.

Page 59
1. Franklin D. Roosevelt.
2. July–October 1940.
3. Henry Moore – you can see his drawings at the Imperial War Museum.

Page 60
1. It was used to calculate high tide at London Bridge, so people knew when to expect guests coming up river to the palace.
2. It was invented in Denmark by Ole Kirk Christiansen in 1932.
3. Real tennis.

QUICK QUIZ

❶ St. Stephen's Tower
❷ Yellow
❸ The Angel of Charity
❹ The Natural History Museum
❺ Fruit and vegetable
❻ 12.5 miles (20 km)
❼ The Queen's official birthday
❽ Kensington Gardens and Hyde Park
❾ The Battle of Trafalgar
❿ Six months
⓫ Whipsnade Zoo
⓬ Apollo 10
⓭ The British Museum
⓮ Leicester Square
⓯ Brown, sand tiger, and nurse sharks
⓰ 1972
⓱ A penny plain, two pence colored
⓲ Sir Christopher Wren
⓳ 1662
⓴ A Yeoman Warder
The Big Ben clocktower is 320 ft (106 m) tall.